Colonial Leaders

WITHDRAWN

Increase Mather

Clergyman and Scholar

Colonial Leaders

Lord Baltimore
English Politician and Colonist

Benjamin Banneker
American Mathematician and Astronomer

Sir William Berkeley
Governor of Virginia

William Bradford
Governor of Plymouth Colony

Jonathan Edwards
Colonial Religious Leader

Benjamin Franklin
American Statesman, Scientist, and Writer

Anne Hutchinson
Religious Leader

Cotton Mather
Author, Clergyman, and Scholar

Increase Mather
Clergyman and Scholar

James Oglethorpe
Humanitarian and Soldier

William Penn
Founder of Democracy

Sir Walter Raleigh
English Explorer and Author

Caesar Rodney
American Patriot

John Smith
English Explorer and Colonist

Miles Standish
Plymouth Colony Leader

Peter Stuyvesant
Dutch Military Leader

George Whitefield
Clergyman and Scholar

Roger Williams
Founder of Rhode Island

John Winthrop
Politician and Statesman

John Peter Zenger
Free Press Advocate

Revolutionary War Leaders

John Adams
Second U.S. President

Ethan Allen
Revolutionary Hero

Benedict Arnold
Traitor to the Cause

King George III
English Monarch

Nathanael Greene
Military Leader

Nathan Hale
Revolutionary Hero

Alexander Hamilton
First U.S. Secretary of the Treasury

John Hancock
President of the Continental Congress

Patrick Henry
American Statesman and Speaker

John Jay
First Chief Justice of the Supreme Court

Thomas Jefferson
Author of the Declaration of Independence

John Paul Jones
Father of the U.S. Navy

Lafayette
French Freedom Fighter

James Madison
Father of the Constitution

Francis Marion
The Swamp Fox

James Monroe
American Statesman

Thomas Paine
Political Writer

Paul Revere
American Patriot

Betsy Ross
American Patriot

George Washington
First U.S. President

Famous Figures of the Civil War Era

Jefferson Davis
Confederate President

Frederick Douglass
Abolitionist and Author

Ulysses S. Grant
Military Leader and President

Stonewall Jackson
Confederate General

Robert E. Lee
Confederate General

Abraham Lincoln
Civil War President

William Sherman
Union General

Harriet Beecher Stowe
Author of Uncle Tom's Cabin

Sojourner Truth
Abolitionist, Suffragist, and Preacher

Harriet Tubman
Leader of the Underground Railroad

Increase Mather

Clergyman and Scholar

Norma Jean Lutz

Arthur M. Schlesinger, jr.
Senior Consulting Editor

Chelsea House Publishers

Philadelphia

Produced by Pre-Press Company, Inc., East Bridgewater, MA 02333

CHELSEA HOUSE PUBLISHERS
Editor in Chief Stephen Reginald
Production Manager Pamela Loos
Art Director Sara Davis
Director of Photography Judy L. Hasday
Managing Editor James D. Gallagher
Senior Production Editor J. Christopher Higgins

Staff for *INCREASE MATHER*
Project Editor Anne Hill
Associate Art Director Takeshi Takahashi
Series Design Keith Trego

The Chelsea House World Wide Web address is http://www.chelseahouse.com

First Printing
1 3 5 7 9 8 6 4 2

Library of Congress Cataloging-in-Publication Data

Lutz, Norma Jean
    Increase Mather/Norma Jean Lutz.
        p. cm.—(Colonial leaders)
    Includes bibliographical references (p.).
    ISBN 0-7910-5962-6 (HC); 0-7910-6119-1 (PB)
    1. Mather, Increase, 1639–1723—Juvenile literature.
    2. Puritans—Massachusetts—Biography—Juvenile literature.
    3. Massachusetts—History—Colonial period, ca. 1600–1775—Juvenile
    literature. [1. Mather, Increase, 1639–1723. 2. Puritans.] I. Title. II. Series.

F67 .M4738 2000
285.8'092—dc21
[B]
                                                    00-035848

Publisher's Note: In Colonial and Revolutionary War America, there were no standard rules for spelling, punctuation, capitalization, or grammar. Some of the quotations that appear in the Colonial Leaders and Revolutionary War Leaders series come from original documents and letters written during this time in history. Original quotations reflect writing inconsistencies of the period.

Contents

When Richard Mather and his family
arrived in Boston, the harbor was
surrounded by tall fences to keep out
wolves. Boston Harbor would later
develop into a bustling commercial center
for the colonies.

1

The Mathers in the New World

The Mather family was one of the most famous in all of New England. For three generations they had played major roles in the political as well as religious life of the Massachusetts Bay Colony. It all began with Richard, who was born in England in 1596.

As a boy, Richard Mather received an education when schooling and studies were not the common practice. At the young age of 15 he became a full-fledged schoolmaster. While teaching, he lived with a religious family named Aspinwall. While living with the Aspinwalls, Richard became aware of his sinfulness and learned of the saving power of God as preached by the Puritans.

Puritans were people who felt the ceremonies of the Church of England were devised by men and were not from the Bible. Therefore, they believed that those rules and ceremonies need not be obeyed by those who feared God. They believed in strictly following the teachings of the Bible.

Richard later studied at Oxford and then began preaching. Because of his Puritan beliefs, he was at odds with the king, who demanded that all preachers conform to the teachings of the Church of England. Courageously, Richard stood firm for what he believed was right, and he was eventually suspended from preaching. As a consequence, he gathered his family and left his homeland. In the New World, in the area known as New England, they hoped to worship freely.

On June 4, 1635, Richard Mather, his wife Katherine, and their four sons (the eldest was only nine), boarded the ship *James* in Bristol, England. They sailed for 75 days. At one point, they narrowly escaped shipwreck. They went ashore in Boston on August 17.

Richard Mather's reputation preceded him. Many New England churches invited him to become their pastor. He decided to live in Dorchester, a mile away from Boston. There, he served the 30 or so members in a little meetinghouse at the corner of Cottage and Pleasant Streets.

In their new home in Dorchester, two more sons were born: Eleazar in 1637 and on June 21, 1639, their youngest son, Increase. Two days after his birth, Increase was baptized at the Dorchester church. He was so named because of the great prosperity that England saw in the 1600s. Being strong in their faith, his parents felt it was their duty to name their son Increase so as to never forget the blessings they enjoyed.

Of all the sons born to Richard and Katherine Mather, it would be Increase who most closely carried on his father's work. And

Increase would be the one who would rise to power through a long and active life in Boston.

At the time when Increase was born, Boston and the surrounding communities numbered less than 5,000 people.

Fishing boats were moored in the harbor, and stacks of furs from Indian traders could be seen lying about. Tall fences built to ward off the wolves were a constant reminder that this settlement was at the very edge of the wilderness. One could see the bare beginnings of roads that connected the outlying communities.

While the Puritans were known to write detailed biographies, very little emphasis was placed on childhood, and therefore, we have no details about Increase as a small child. We do, however, know much about the circumstances that surrounded him during this time.

A number of university-trained Puritan men had arrived in Boston before the Mathers. By the time Increase was born, Puritan thinking and Puritan rule were firmly established. The community, the church, and the government were built upon biblical principles. Ministers were considered leaders not only in the church but leaders in the community and in government affairs.

Increase's father was definitely one of these well-respected leaders. As the son of such a leader, Increase was no doubt present when important church and civic meetings were held in the Mathers' home. With the help of Reverend John Eliot and Reverend Thomas Weld, his father had translated the Psalms into English meter for singing. This was called the *Bay Psalm Book,* and was the first book printed in America. At every Sunday service in the Dorchester meetinghouse, Increase sang from the book his father had helped write. He listened to his father preach powerful sermons. He saw the high respect that his father commanded from all the **parishioners.**

When Increase was only seven, his father served as a leader in the **synod** of 1646. This council of churches came together to write out a model platform for church government called the *Cambridge Platform*. Many of Richard Mather's ideas were used in the final document. This manual of rules for the Congregational Church was used for more than 100 years.

Increase's older brothers attended Harvard, after which two decided to return to England. We can imagine that the letters from these brothers were filled with important news—such as the execution of King Charles I in 1648.

While some have portrayed Puritans as being stiff and unfeeling, we know that Increase grew up with the love and tender affection of caring parents. There is nothing in his later diaries which indicates that Richard and Katherine were anything but doting. In his father's study and at his mother's knee, he learned to read and write. When he was nine, he attended a schoolhouse near the church. His schoolmaster was a man named Henry Butler. By the time Increase turned twelve, whether he enjoyed the exercises or not, he was able to write and speak fluent

Latin, and he knew Greek as well.

Many bookshops and printing shops could be found in Boston at this time, and books, pamphlets, and almanacs were constantly being added to the young boy's growing library. One such book, in which he wrote his name and dated it 1651, was an analysis of the Ten Commandments written by a bishop of the Church of England. Perhaps it was a gift from his father as Increase prepared to go away to college at the early age of 12.

The first book printed in America was a translation of the Psalms into English. Richard Mather developed this book for use in religious services.

Increase admitted in later years that, "Until I was fourteen years old, I had no love to, nor delight in my books." In spite of this fact, he led his class at Harvard. The college, located across the Charles River in Cambridge, was nothing like modern college campuses of today.

The Harvard of Increase's day consisted of one building (in need of repair) and a notable lack of books. Students looked out their windows onto a large plain more than eight miles square. Finances to support the school were always meager. Every family in the commonwealth was encouraged to donate pecks of wheat and bushels of corn to "maintain poor scholars at Cambridge" and "for the advancement of learning."

The school records show that one student balanced his accounts with pork, wheat, corn, meal, hens, eggs, boars, sheep, calves, lambs, beef, and silver. "A blacke Cow" and "a fatt Cow" from a man named George Babcock enabled the two Mather brothers, Eleazar and Increase, to attend school. We can assume that Mr. Babcock must have owed a debt to Reverend Richard Mather, and his debt in turn paid the tuition.

College life must have been a big change for a 12-year-old leaving home for the first time. Rules were strict and unbending. Students were to report to their tutors twice each day. No public meetings were allowed among the student body. All students were required to speak Latin during school hours. Punishment for disobedience consisted of fines, public scoldings, whippings, and what was called "tucking"–having the chin pinched with a thumbnail until blood came.

Increase's studies centered around **theology** with only a smattering of science, and nothing of the arts. He was particularly impressed by Reverend John Cotton, an instructor and a friend of his father. Cotton died when Increase was still a student at Harvard. (In later years, after Increase's father was widowed, he would marry John Cotton's widow.)

During Increase's time at Harvard, the president, Henry Dunster, added a fourth year to the course. This angered many students, 17 of

One man who had impressed Increase Mather during his study of theology was Reverend John Cotton, an instructor and family friend. Increase would later marry his daughter, Maria Cotton, and one of their sons was Cotton Mather.

whom left without taking their degrees. Increase's parents insisted that he graduate. They did, however, remove Increase from the campus and arranged for him to study under John Norton. Norton served as minister at the church in Ipswich. In the Norton home, Increase thrived. While the Reverend Norton helped to kindle a blaze of religious devotion in Increase, it was two other events that set his feet in the direction for his life's work.

At age 15, Increase became ill and almost died. He returned to his family home. This frightful experience led him to shut himself up in his father's study where he listed his sins and cried out to God for mercy and forgiveness. He described the outcome in his own words:

> I gave myself up to Jesus Christ, declaring that I was now resolved to be his servant, I his only, and his forever. . . . Upon this I had ease and inward peace in my perplexed soul immediately.

The following year, he faced the death of his beloved mother. As she lay dying, her last request to her youngest son was that he enter the ministry.

These two events crystallized his purpose and determined his life's work. By the time he graduated from Harvard, August 12, 1656, Increase knew he was to follow in his father's footsteps. He knew he would serve God and preach the Gospel.

In 1657, Increase Mather went to England after graduating from Harvard College. The England that he arrived in was far different than the one his father had left 20 years earlier.

Increase in England

Upon his 18th birthday, Increase preached his first sermon in his father's church in Dorchester. He chose as his text the scripture in the book of Genesis: "And Enoch walked with God: and he was not; for God took him."

It was during this time that the widower, Richard Mather, took the widow of John Cotton for his wife. Into the Mather household also came John Cotton's daughter, Maria, who would later become Mrs. Increase Mather.

We find no record as to how Increase occupied his time during the year or so following his graduation.

We do know that his thoughts were turning to England. There, his brother Nathaniel was at Barnstaple in Devonshire, and Samuel served as a minister in Dublin, Ireland. It was Samuel who encouraged Increase to come to him.

Many young Harvard graduates traveled back to England and Ireland, due to the opportunities of higher learning there. The older colleges with their well-stocked library shelves drew those who hungered to study more. Trinity College in Dublin leaned toward Puritan teachings, which certainly appealed to Increase. To be surrounded by those who thought as he did, including his own brother, might prove a good place to launch his career.

On July 3, 1657, Increase boarded a ship bound for England. He and his father wept at their parting. Sailing in those days was extremely risky, and neither knew if they would ever see each other again. The five-week voyage gave the young man plenty of time to think about his life and future plans.

The England that Increase came to was much different than the one his father had left years earlier. The Puritans were now in power and the English church had given way to the beliefs and dictates of the Puritans.

Increase arrived in Portsmouth and traveled to London and on to Lancashire where he stayed with friends of his father. In early autum he sailed for Dublin. Increase had not seen his brother, Samuel, for eight years. Because Samuel did not recognize him, Increase had to be introduced by the letters he brought along.

Increase was quickly enrolled, along with 200 other

Ships in the 17th century were not designed for comfort. Passengers lived in cramped quarters with barely enough room to stand up. Many passengers became seasick due to the pitching and rolling of the ship. The conditions were filthy, and diseases such as measles and smallpox were common.

In these tight quarters, passengers had to find room for their belongings— wooden chests, iron pots, tools, and baby cradles. In rough weather, these items would knock about making conditions even worse.

Food consisted of dried beef, smoked fish, cheese, and dried biscuits (hardtack).

students, at Trinity College. Rules at Trinity were as strict as Harvard, and the curriculum was similar as well. The difference came in the library filled with 4,000 books, which must have seemed to Increase like a wide open door of opportunity.

His first year at Trinity was filled with problems. He first became ill with the measles, followed by a bout of smallpox. Then came the most severe winter ever known in Ireland. That he survived was amazing, but by the following June he had completed his course and received his master of arts degree from Trinity.

At the ceremony, Increase showed true Mather spirit by refusing to wear the cap (or hood). He even succeeded in convincing at least one other graduate to join him. The act did not hinder his being invited to become a **fellow** of the college. He did not accept this offer, but instead accepted a position to become a preacher in a small Ulster town. However, on the way he became ill and had to return to Dublin. Once there, he struggled through two more severe ill-

Increase traveled to Ireland to continue his education at Trinity College in Dublin. The damp Irish air did not agree with him, however, and a series of illnesses forced him to return to England.

nesses. At last, he decided the damp Irish air did not agree with him; he would return to England.

Arriving in London in July 1658, he met John Howe, a man well-known throughout England as someone who had favor with Oliver Cromwell. (Cromwell, a Puritan, had become Lord Protector of England in 1653 and ruled the country with an iron hand.) Appointed to a high post near Cromwell's side, Howe was forced to leave his position of preaching at the Great Torrington Church in Devonshire.

John Howe saw great promise in Increase Mather and invited him to substitute for him at Torrington. For the next few months, Increase divided his time between preaching at Torrington and staying with his brother Nathaniel, a preacher at Barnstaple, nine miles away.

When Oliver Cromwell died in September of 1658, circumstances quickly changed. Cromwell's son, Richard, was a weak leader. This allowed King Charles II to return home from exile and eventually regain the throne. John Howe, of course, had to return to his church at Torrington. This meant Increase was no longer needed there. However, through Nathaniel's connections of friends, a position was established for Increase on the island of Guernsey.

Guernsey is part of the Channel Islands, a cluster of islands located in the English Channel between England and France. There, Increase preached every Sunday morning. In the afternoons, he rowed back to shore to hold services in the town church at Petersport. Due to its location, the people of Guernsey followed French traditions and customs that the young Puritan preacher found peculiar. His stay there, however, was a short one.

This appeared to be a restless time in Increase's life. It's not clear whether it was due to his youth or to the conditions of unrest in the country. He desired to return to Dublin, but Samuel discouraged it. Then came an invitation from James

Puritan Oliver Cromwell raised up an army to defeat Charles I in a civil war. After the king was beheaded, Cromwell became Lord Protector of England.

Although Cromwell was a great military commander, he knew little about politics. He searched for a form of government that might please all Englishmen. During his reign, Sunday became a day of prayer and recreation was strictly forbidden. Because he did not know how to govern, he became a virtual dictator.

Cromwell was succeeded by his son, Richard, who was more inept than his father. In 1660, Charles II was brought home from exile to take the throne.

Forbes, a minister in Gloucester. Increase readily accepted this position. On December 18, Increase sailed once more for England.

In Gloucester, he lived in the home of James Forbes, a courageous Puritan who continued to preach in the face of danger to his own life. On Sunday mornings, Increase preached in the church of St. Mary-de-Lode, which was located just outside the cathedral gate. However, on Sunday afternoons he was granted the privilege of preaching inside the great historic cathedral itself. This cathedral boasted the largest window in England, measuring 38 by 78 feet. Inside, the cathedral columns, which were 7 feet in diameter, rose to heights of 32 feet.

What a striking contrast this was to the small, stark meetinghouses back in New England. In this magnificent setting, Increase prepared to settle down. He looked forward to working alongside Forbes to build up the congregation. But it wasn't to be. With the return of the royal rule in England, Puritans would be required to be loyal to the Crown. Reluctantly, he left Gloucester to return to the island of Guernsey. In nearby Petersport, England, on May 31, 1660, Charles II was officially crowned the king.

In the midst of the rejoicing and celebrations for the new king, Increase Mather refused to drink to the king's health. He then refused to sign papers of allegiance and urged others to follow his stand. Although he was able to continue preaching, he was forced to do so without pay. By March 1661, a

When Increase refused to drink to the health of the new king (pictured above) or to sign papers of allegiance to the royal government, he was forced to leave the town where he was preaching.

new governor was appointed to Guernsey who insisted on strict conformity. Increase would either have to obey, or leave. In his journal he recorded:

> Sir Hugh Pollard being made Governor It was now come to that, that I must either leave Guernsey or conform to the ceremonies of the church of England so that I tooke my leave of that Island.

Returning to Weymouth and Dorchester, he continued to preach. He worked with small independent congregations, helping them to remain strong in spite of the persecution. Many of these services were held in homes so as to be undetected. Among the leaders whom Increase assisted was John Wesley. (In years to come, Wesley's grandson of the same name, would become the founder of the Methodist Church in New England.)

Increase's days of preaching in large, beautiful churches in England were over. Puritan supremacy was over. Money was offered to him to conform to the demands of the Crown, but he refused to do so. He considered going to Holland, where Nathaniel had escaped to, but those plans came to nothing. Almost as a last resort, he began to think of returning to his birthplace. This plan was not his first choice, for he had come to love England dearly. Thus, when he embarked for Boston on June 29, 1661, it was not a trip he eagerly anticipated. Rather, he did so "with submission to the will of God."

Increase had left America as a boy, but he returned as a man who had been tested and held true to what he believed. He'd traveled all across the British Isles, from the bustling streets of London to the quiet Devonshire hillsides. People with whom he had studied and worked would forever have a place in his heart.

His ship anchored in Newfoundland and from there, he boarded yet another ship to travel to Boston. In his autobiography he writes that he wept for joy upon seeing his beloved father once again. This, he writes, was "the first, & I think the only time that I ever wept for joy."

In spite of all the disappointments, he was thankful to be home.

Upon his return to Boston, Increase noticed that great changes had taken place in Boston, especially along the harbor and waterfront. The peaceful shores had given way to bustling wharves and countinghouses.

A Leader in Boston

The first Sunday following his arrival home, Increase Mather and his brother Eleazar led the services in their father's church.

> [H]earing his two Sons, in his own Pulpit entertain the People of GOD, with Performances, that made all People Proclaim him, An Happy Father.

The town of Boston had grown a great deal since Increase had been away. Wooden wharves now stretched long fingers out into the bay. All along the wharves were warehouses and places of business called **countinghouses.** Here, Boston's shipping

Clerks employed in the countinghouses worked a 12-hour day, six days a week. Some were apprentices and shared quarters above the countinghouses.

Floors were swept, brass doorknobs and handles were shined. Fires were stoked, quills sharpened, and inkwells filled. During the day, clerks took the account books and the correspondence books from desk to desk. Four copies were made of each document, and the chief clerk watched to see that no mistakes were made.

Breakfast consisted of tea and a piece of johnnycake. Lunch might be codfish stew. Wages were no more than five or six shillings a week—with no time off.

industry, in its infancy, was taking hold and growing. A public library was in the planning stages, and many of the dirt streets were neatly paved with pebble stone. However, to a man who had known the sprawling, crowded streets of London, Boston must have paled in comparison.

During his first few months home, Increase received no less than six invitations from area churches to fill their pulpits. For a time, his attention was drawn to his father's home in Dorchester. His stepsister Maria Cotton, whom he now courted, lived there. The two were married in

March 1662. Increase and his new bride moved into the home of her deceased father, John Cotton. Maria lived as a married woman in the very house in which she was born.

There is no record of their young love because Puritan training did not encourage romantic expression. We can only wonder if Increase's thoughts turned often to Maria during his years away from Boston. His later writings, however, tell of a deep, abiding love between the two. About his Maria, Increase would write that the Lord gave him "a great Blessing," and a "Dear Companion of" his "Pilgrimage on Earth."

The following year, on February 12, Maria gave birth to their first child, a son. Three days later, at the infant's baptism in the meetinghouse, he was given the name of Cotton, after his grandfather, John Cotton. As Increase had followed in his own father's footsteps, so too would Cotton Mather.

Increase moved quickly into a place of leadership. In 1662, he was called upon to serve as a delegate in the synod which adopted the Half-Way Covenant. This **covenant** had to do with rules of church membership. Originally, only adults were granted membership. Children were required to give an account of salvation before they could be accepted as a member. For some, this never happened.

Questions arose when these "half-members" then had children: should the third-generation children be allowed to be baptized and take **communion?** The synod finally agreed that the **unregenerate** members could receive baptism and membership but not participate in the Lord's Supper or in church elections. This created two classes of membership: **communicants** (one who takes communion) and noncommunicants.

Heated arguments arose over the issue. Obviously, if children were not baptized, eventually there would be more nonmembers in the church than members.

Increase was set against his own father in the matter. While Richard Mather favored the Half-

Way Covenant, Increase opposed it, feeling it would lower the standards of the church.

While the majority was in favor, the minority did not remain silent. The president of the synod, Charles Chauncy, agreed with Increase and printed a protest against the synod's decision. Increase wrote the preface to the essay. This preface, which became his first published work, pointed out the danger of "great Corruption and Pollution creeping into the Churches, by the Enlargement of Baptism."

It took courage for young Mather to oppose not only his father but a number of the elder leaders. His writing was in no way a hotheaded attack; it was a calm, clear presentation of what he felt was right. Considering the circumstances, it was amazing that Increase and his father remained close friends.

By 1668, however, Increase had changed his mind about the strict doctrine of baptism. Actual experience as a church pastor helped him be more practical. While some have taught that the

Puritan fathers were unbending and rigid in all beliefs, this change of heart by Increase proved that it was not always the case.

During the first months after his return, Increase alternately preached in Second Church in Boston, as well as in his father's church in Dorchester. His diaries, which he began keeping at this time, recorded his struggle as to whether he should accept a call from Second Church. There, he would serve as the assistant to the pastor, John Mayo.

The decision finally made, he broke off with his father's church and was admitted to the Boston church on March 10, 1664. On May 24, he was formally installed as a teacher and received his charge from the hands of his father. Thus his life's course was set—he would spend the remainder of his life working at Second Church.

A man who loved home and family, Increase especially enjoyed spending hours in his study. His library contained nearly 700 volumes, many of which were Bible commentaries and sermons. There were, however, books on science as well. "I have ever since any of you can remember," he told his children, "loved to be in no place on the Earth, so much as in my Study."

Increase's elderly father, Richard Mather, died in April 1669, bringing great grief to Increase. This great leader, who had preached to his Dorchester congregation for more than 50 years, seemed to be the ideal Puritan. Barely three months later, Increase's close brother, Eleazar, died in Northampton.

Following the two deaths, Increase attempted to assist not only his father's congregation but his deceased brother's as well. Perhaps it was the grief in addition to the extra workload that caused him to become ill. For many days he lay near death. After his recuperation, his brush with death caused him to desire to do something that would remain after he was gone. He set about planning what books he would write, beginning with the biography of Richard Mather. The biography was published in Cambridge in

1670 and was dedicated to his father's congregation in Dorchester.

As John Mayo grew old and infirm, he gave more church responsibilities to Increase. In order to better handle this work, Increase moved his family to a house located just across from the church at North Square. By now the family had grown to include another son, Nathaniel, and two daughters, Maria and Elizabeth. In the new home another daughter, Sarah, was born in 1671, followed by a son, Samuel, in 1674.

The reputation of Increase grew throughout Boston and the surrounding towns. He was sought out for counsel and his many writings were purchased and discussed in places of business and in meeting halls. Two duties came to him that reinforced this community trust. On May 27, 1674, Increase Mather was licensed to regulate a printing press in the city of Boston. Knowing the power of the printed word, the colonies held control over the presses. Mather kept the printing under the wing of Harvard College.

The second trust that came to Increase Mather was the presidency of Harvard College. It was an office he did not seek. In fact, he turned down the invitation twice before finally accepting the post. He first served as an elected fellow in 1675, and finally, with reluctance, accepted full leadership in 1685.

He had no thought of leaving Boston to assume the presidential duties. As he continued to devote his time to his church, he rode on horseback out to Cambridge once or twice a week, taking the Charlestown ferry. Under his guidance, the school flourished.

The first modern university was established in Bologna, Italy, in 1088 as a law school. Other cities began to copy the system. The University of Paris was founded in 1150; England's Oxford University was founded in 1187. Harvard, the first university in America, was founded in 1636.

The basic structure has remained unchanged through the centuries. A prescribed curriculum is taught by licensed instructors. Scholars take formal examinations and then are granted degrees that show they have finished their course in a satisfactory manner.

In past centuries, classes were taught in Latin and students were required to speak Latin.

He encouraged the study of science and medicine. He sought to expand the curriculum beyond just the training of ministers.

A dark shadow of concern to all in the colonies occurred as relationships with the Indians began to weaken. The Indians, once friendly under the leadership of Massasoit, saw their land gradually being taken from them. Their discontent finally exploded into violence. A number of towns in Massachusetts were attacked and many settlers killed. Increase took it upon himself to write a history, entitled "A Brief History of the War with the Indians." This was the first essay he wrote that was not theological.

As the citizens of Boston were still in mourning for the loss of their dead, a severe epidemic hit, resulting in more deaths. Then, on November 27, 1676, the Mathers' home and the church were destroyed in a fire. By the time the fire was stopped (a welcome rain helped douse the flames), a large part of North Boston had been

Increase Mather served as an elected fellow to Harvard in 1675 and reluctantly accepted a position as president in 1685. The school flourished under his guidance, and he often encouraged the students to study science and medicine in addition to their training as ministers.

destroyed. To Increase Mather's great relief, no lives were lost and his books were saved.

If this did not present problems enough, in the same year, England sent to the colonies a

Metacom (or Metacomet) was the second son of Massasoit, chief of the Wampanoag Confederacy. Massasoit had been friends with the Pilgrims. Metacom was given the English name of Philip; his older brother became Alexander.

In anger, Philip turned against the English. He created an alliance of Indians to fight the settlers. The settlers gave the nickname "King Philip" to the Wampanoag Indian.

The bloody war that followed was led by King Philip. Indians burned settlements, killing men, women, and children. The colonists attempted to fight back but were not prepared to fight a war.

special messenger of the Crown, Edward Randolph. Randolph, much disliked by the colonists, attempted to bring the Church of England into power in the colonies. His desire was to open the Puritan meetinghouse to all who would be admitted to the English church. This was the very rule that the Puritans had come to America to escape.

Randolph also made a series of accusations, one of which was that English citizens had been executed in Massachusetts because of their religious beliefs. This made the colonies look very bad in the eyes of English royalty, and therefore, was hotly contested by the Puritans.

All of the Massachusetts Bay Colony functioned under a **charter** that had been granted them in 1629. This charter served for over 50 years as the constitution for the self-governing colony. Now, that freedom was being threatened and action had to be taken.

King Philip was hunted down in a swamp in Rhode Island and killed on August 12, 1676.

Known throughout England for its lavish
furnishings and paintings, the Banqueting
House at Whitehall Palace was the site of
many social events held by the English
royal family.

Diplomat to England

The population of Boston was becoming more varied than ever before. Many of the citizens who lived there were not influenced by clergymen such as Increase Mather. So when a "declaration" came from England in October 1683, the reactions were as varied as the people it affected.

This declaration promised that if the colony would submit to the will of the king, he would regulate the charter in the way that seemed best to him. On January 21, at a crowded gathering at the townhouse, Mather urged the people to send representatives to England to defend their original charter. After his

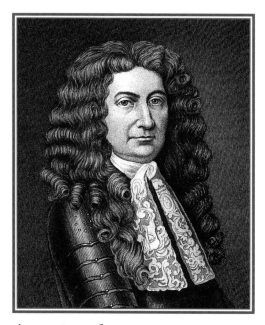

Appointed as governor of the Massachusetts Bay Colony in 1684, Sir Edmund Andros was an unsympathetic leader who increased fees and often demanded the use of the churches for nonreligious purposes.

moving speech, the colony voted unanimously to reject the declaration.

The courageous action of these citizens ushered in a time of turbulence and unrest in the colonies. Just one year later, the Crown declared the old charter of Massachusetts to be **invalid.** The colony came under the rule of men appointed by the king. Some of these leaders were sympathetic to the needs and desires of the colonists. Among those who were not was Sir Edmund Andros, who was appointed governor.

Under the rule of Andros, official fees were increased, all legal business was moved to Boston, and land titles were up for dispute.

Every land owner was required to have his hold-
ings **validated**—and the fees were substantial.
Andros and his council had power to impose
taxes as they wished. The most serious problem,
however, lay with church business. Andros
brought to New England the same power that
had once persecuted Puritans in England.

Problems in the land did not distract Increase
from his own church. He continued to write, turning out eight new books between 1683 and 1688.
Increase's son, Cotton, was ordained and came to
work by his father's side. This both lightened Increase's load and gave him great peace and joy.

Great tact was required of a man like Increase Mather during the rule of Andros as governor. Andros began to demand the use of one
of the Boston churches in which to hold an English service. At one point he forced his way into
a meetinghouse and used it against the wishes of
those who attended there.

In 1687, King James issued a declaration of
liberty for all faiths, encouraging tolerance of

worship in Massachusetts. Rather than seeing this as a threat, Increase Mather looked upon it as a way to talk with the king. He suggested to other Boston ministers that an expression of their thanks be sent to King James. In favor of the idea, they selected Mather as the one to go to England.

When Edward Randolph got word of this possibility, he attempted to arrest Increase Mather. This forced Increase to go into hiding. After he learned of two failed arrest attempts, Increase decided to leave for England. On March 30, disguised in a white robe and a white wig, he slipped out of his house after dark. Randolph's guards did not recognize Mather.

He made his way to a friend's home in Charlestown. Later he was met by his younger son, Samuel, and the two traveled at night to Plymouth. Hiding in a small boat in the harbor, they waited for word that the ship on which they had paid passage, had sailed. The smaller boat then took them quickly out to the bigger ship. There Mather and Samuel clambered safely aboard.

England, at this time, was ruled by James II who was attempting to make all of England Catholic. The Catholics were distrusted by both the Church of England and the Puritans. In spite of the fact that Increase Mather was not a lawyer, he showed amazing skill and wisdom in dealing with delicate matters of the king's court. Within a few days of arriving in England, he was presented to the king. Formerly, Increase had been a

In 1687, King James II issued a declaration which encouraged tolerance of worship in Massachusetts.

person who defied royalty and opposed Catholics. Putting these thoughts aside, he met with the king using polite diplomacy. Mather brought to the king not only praise and thanks from the colonies, but many strong complaints against Andros. The king asked Mather to put his

The Banqueting House of Whitehall Palace is well-known for its architecture and paintings. However, it is most famous for the event that took place on January 30, 1649. Here, on a scaffold set up against the outer walls, Charles I was beheaded in front of thousands of onlookers.

In 1654, Oliver Cromwell made the palace his official residence. When Charles II came to power in 1660, he made a triumphal procession through the London streets to the Banqueting House. The Banqueting House then reverted to its use as a ceremonial chamber where grand receptions were held—and are still held today.

requests in writing, which he did quickly.

During his stay, Increase met with many influential people, not only Puritans but members of the royal court. He sought their guidance. He met with nobles, lords, ladies, and other religious leaders. He became well-known all over London. He kept busy not only by writing but by serving as guest preacher in a number of pulpits.

Among those he met was Sir William Phips, a New Englander who had found financial success by retrieving sunken treasures from the sea. His wealth caused him to be knighted by the king. He maintained an interest in New England and had a home in Boston. He was opposed to Andros and wanted to help Increase Mather in getting rid of the cruel leader. It was not the last interaction Mather would have with Phips.

Mather's petitions to the king did not ask for church **sovereignty** in New England. He was wise enough to know that times were changing and that neither his own church nor his **sect** could hold all the power in the fast-growing colony. His requests were for a democracy that allowed little power or rule from the Crown. Negotiations were progressing well, until word came of a possible uprising against the king.

English citizens who feared Catholic rule had appealed to Mary, James's daughter, and her husband William, a duke from Holland, to take the throne. By December 1688, William and Mary were safely in Whitehall being congratulated by their new subjects who welcomed their rule. Now it appeared Increase Mather would have to begin all over again with his negotiations.

When news of England's uprising reached New England, the colonists realized that the ruling force that had appointed Andros was no longer in power. Since Mather's departure, Governor Andros had expanded his powers even more. The colonists seized this opportunity. Overjoyed, they rose up against Andros, arrested him, and set in place their own provincial government.

Back in England, Increase learned that King William was not as easy to work with as James had been. William had no reason to be kind to a nonconformist like Increase Mather. In addition, the king was distracted by other affairs, such as dealing with a rebellion in Ireland and visiting his lands in Holland. In spite of these setbacks, Increase wasted no time in presenting the needs of New England to the king. He also won an audience with the queen and gained her acceptance.

The time was approaching for Mather to return to Boston and attend the needs of the colony. A corporation bill was referred to a committee which would result in a favorable

When William landed in England and took the throne, Mather had to begin his appeal process over again.

charter for New England. The king had ordered the return of Andros and Randolph to England. Things were falling into place, when suddenly Increase's plans were changed. Just as he and his son were preparing to leave, Samuel came down with smallpox. The two Mathers were forced to return to London.

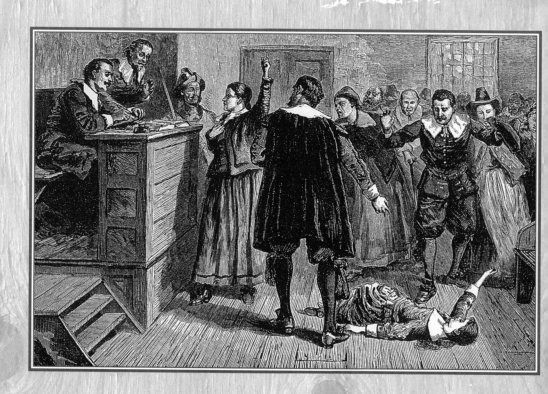

Governor Phips and Increase Mather faced a very difficult situation in Salem Village. A number of citizens had been accused of practicing witchcraft and were placed on trial and executed in various tests designed to prove they were witches.

Troubles in the Colonies

It is difficult to know what might have happened if Increase had been able to return home at that moment. As it was, the tide of events now turned against him.

In **Parliament,** the **Whigs** and **Tories** disputed over matters concerning New England. This caused a delay in the approval of the charter, giving time for enemies of the cause to gain a foothold. Andros and Randolph arrived in England, after which Mather and his associates were forced to appear with them before a royal committee. The colonists saw that it was useless to continue to press charges against Andros since they had no viable proof against him. Andros had many friends in England and was presented with a skillful defense. Randolph continued to viciously attack New England for such things as violating English trade laws.

With no one to sign charges against him, Andros went free. This weakened the stand Mather had taken. Mather and his associates now found themselves on the defensive. Throughout 1690 few gains were made.

It wasn't until spring of 1691 that William at last gave his attention to the charter. The charter drawn up by the colonists requested that the people of New England be allowed to choose their own leaders and make their own laws. King William did not agree. William's plan was to have a governor appointed by the Crown. The colonists, however, would be allowed to appoint their own representatives for government.

Increase tirelessly reviewed each draft of the charter, asking for changes and suggesting revisions. He was successful in protecting colonists' titles to their own land, which had been threatened by the tyrant Andros. On September 17, the Privy Council ordered the secretary to "prepare a warrant for his Majesty's royal signature for passing said charter." This charter became the new document under which the colonists would live. Sir William Phips was selected as governor, which, at the time, pleased Mather.

With the charter signed and finished, Mather's work was completed. On March 29, 1792, he sailed for home with his son Samuel and the newly appointed governor.

The new charter would be received with mixed responses. There were benefits such as the right to elect representatives, but the power of a Crown-appointed governor disappointed many.

While Increase may have failed to accomplish what some would have liked to have had in a new charter, he succeeded in many other ways. Without his diplomatic presence, his close attention to detail, and his tireless efforts, the charter may not have been as kind as it was. Mather knew and understood that as long as there was a king in England, the colonies would be subject to his rule. It was best to work with those who were in control.

Increase Mather became the first foreign diplomat for the colonies. He demonstrated to England that the colonists had well-defined aims and skilled, educated men to speak for them. Increase Mather's writing style which had before been mainly theological, also lent itself to writing political pamphlets.

While in London, he conversed with scientists and astrologers. He studied books of science, broadening his knowledge beyond that of a mere preacher. Many of the new books which appeared in his Boston library were purchased during his stay in England. Increase Mather had been willing to part from his dear family, his beloved congregation, and his preaching to take on this five-year work to gain the new charter.

Arriving in Boston on May 14, 1692, the new governor was greeted with eight companies of militia. The military escort marched with Mather and Phips to the Phips's home, which would now become the governor's mansion. Increase and Samuel then returned home where they were happily greeted by Maria and the other siblings.

The new governor was immediately faced with serious problems in a town called Salem Village, located just outside Salem proper, about 14 miles from Boston. Locked in the Salem Village jail were a number of citizens charged with witchcraft, a practice that was against the law in New England.

In the 1600s, belief in the existence of witches was commonplace, not only among the uneducated, but among political officials, scientists, physicians, and the clergy. Even the Royal Society in London held a strong belief in the existence of witches. Strange happenings–things that could not be explained, whether it be an epileptic child or a house that caught fire—were blamed on witches. Such beliefs were not considered superstitions; they were looked upon as facts. In previous years, many witch trials had been held in England, Sweden, and Europe.

The question for the court in Salem Village was not whether there *were* witches, but how to go about proving if a person truly was a witch.

The court that was called to hold the trials in Salem studied cases that had been tried in England. Thinking this was not enough, they turned to the clergy for advice in the matter. They sought counsel from a number of different churches and sects. Increase Mather joined the signers of the ministers who answered the court.

The written answer given by the ministers was filled with pleas for caution. While the ministers believed that the law should be enforced and the court upheld, they advised against accepting "spectral evidence"—taking one person's testimony as fact. In later years, both Increase

Belief in witches was commonplace during the 1600s. People would often accuse their neighbors of practicing witchcraft and turn them over to the village leaders to be put on trial.

and his son Cotton were accused of being responsible for the executions of those accused. However, this was not true. Both Increase and Cotton spoke out against the way that the evidence was handled.

His pamphlet entitled *Cases of Conscience* contains strong language against too much excitement and emotion. In it he states, "there have been ways of trying Witches long used in many Nations . . . which the righteous God never approved of." He spoke out against certain witch tests and called for adequate proof. The courageous Mather summed up by stating, "It were better that ten suspected Witches should escape, than that one innocent Person should be Condemned . . . I had rather judge a Witch to be an honest woman, than judge an honest woman as Witch."

Some historians have said it was because of Mather's writings that the tide of thinking in New England began to turn. Mather himself believed this to be so. In his own diary he wrote:

I doubt [fear] that innocent blood was shed by mistakes . . . I therefore published my Cases of Conscience on witchcrafte, etc. By which (it is sayed) many were enlightened, juries convinced, & the shedding of more innocent blood prevented.

It is clear from these notes that Increase Mather was much more interested in saving innocent lives than in hunting down and convicting those suspected of witchcraft.

One interesting historical note: while witchcraft trials continued in England and Scotland well into the next century, no other witch trial was ever conducted in the colonies.

In his final years, Increase Mather
would resign from Harvard and return
to his beloved church and the comfort
of his own study. At the age of 80,
Mather continued to preach, write,
and provide spiritual guidance for his
congregation.

The Final Years

Up until 1692, Increase Mather held a place of utmost respect, bordering on reverence, among most citizens of Boston and throughout all the colonies. His family grew as his children married and produced a number of grandchildren. He continued with his writing and his studies.

After this time, however, political enemies rose up against him to cause great harm. Elisha Cooke had been with Mather in England and had voted to refuse the charter as it was offered by the king. Upon their return to Massachusetts, Cooke brought criticism against Mather regarding the outcome of the charter. Cooke became the leader of a political faction that opposed Increase Mather and worked to undermine his power. The area they chose to attack Mather was through Harvard College.

Knowing how devoted Mather was to his congregation at Second Church, Cooke and his followers advocated a law that the president of Harvard must live in Cambridge. If Mather refused to leave Boston and his church, Cooke's party could force him to resign as president of the college. If he resigned his church and moved to Cambridge, he could lose his political influence in the largest city in the colonies.

This dilemma was especially painful for Increase Mather. He had not sought the office of president and yet he had sacrificed much time and effort to improve the school. Riding seven or eight miles on horseback in all kinds of New England weather was no small undertaking.

In the end, Mather did indeed get a release from his church and moved to Cambridge.

However, the separation from Boston and all that he'd known for so many decades was more than he could bear. In just over a year, he knew he had been beaten. He resigned the presidency and returned to Boston. Those who had forced the new ruling, found that Mather's successor, Samuel Willard, did not wish to live in Cambridge either. To solve that problem, he was given the title of vice president and allowed to live in Cambridge two days out of the week.

This unfairness grieved Mather greatly. Remembering all he had done for the college, Mather wrote:

> Thus I have been requited by them for all the service I have endeavored to do for them and the Colledge. But why should I think much of it, when Moses, yea, our Lord Himselfe was ill rewarded.

In the end, no real change was made by ousting Mather from the presidency, since Willard's beliefs were essentially the same as Increase

Mather's. Eventually, Elisha Cooke was himself put out of office. Meanwhile, Increase returned to his beloved church, and the comfort of his own study. After Increase's resignation from Harvard, it was his son Cotton who came to the forefront and began fighting the political and religious battles in the colonies.

In 1714, Increase's wife, Maria, died. She had been his partner in the ministry for more than 50 years. In his writings, Increase referred to her as a "Gentlewoman of much Goodness in her Temper; a Godly, an Humble, and a Praying Woman." For five years while he was in England, he trusted her to care for the children and the household, claiming:

> "[M]y heart did safely trust in her, who did me good, & not evil, all the days of my life. She was always very careful not to do anything which she thought would trouble me."

Of his wife's love for him, there can be no doubt, for he wrote:

"[S]he has said to many that she thought I was the best husband, & the best man in the whole world."

In a time when not many people lived to old age, Increase reached the age of 80 in 1720. The thought of death held no terror for him. He looked upon death as his gateway to entry into eternal peace with God. He was, however, still actively writing and preaching. "To preach constantly at fourscore, and to so large an audience, and without notes, is a rare example, and scarcely to be found in history," said one of his friends in England. He attempted to resign, but his congregation begged him to continue–which he did.

By 1722, however, he became too weak to preach any longer. He retired to his home and remained there. On Friday, August 23, he died in the arms of his son, Cotton. His funeral was attended by a "vast number of followers and spectators," among whom were 50 ministers. Many in Britain, as well as in the colonies, grieved his passing.

Increase Mather had been known as a man schooled in theology but whose interests spilled over into literature, education, science, medicine, politics, and public affairs. His books were printed in England, Scotland, and Holland, and they were translated into Dutch, German, French, and Native American languages.

A fellow preacher from Boston, Benjamin Colman, summed it up best when he wrote this of Increase Mather:

> He was the patriarch and prophet among us, if any could be so called: a holy man, and a man of God, holding fast the faithful word, and holding for the word of life. . . . He had also the courage, zeal and boldness of a prophet in what he judged and esteemed to be the cause of God, his truth, his worship and his holiness.

GLOSSARY

charter a written document giving certain rights to people, groups, or organizations

communicant one who takes communion

communion a Christian sacrament of bread or wine that represents the body or blood of Jesus

countinghouse a building or office in which a business firm keeps records of accounts and correspondence

covenant a binding contract between two or more persons or parties

fellow a member of a learned society

invalid not legally valid, not in effect

parishioner a member of a church or parish

parliament an assembly of officials who make the laws for a nation

Puritans a group of English Protestants in the 16th and 17th centuries who wished to simplify ceremonies and creeds of the Church of England

sect a religious body that has separated from a larger denomination

sovereignty supreme authority or rule

synod a council of churches or church officials

theology the study of the nature of God and of man's relationship to God

Tories a political party in England; opponents of the Whigs

unregenerate not spiritually or morally reborn; unrepentant

validate to make official or legal

Whigs a political party in England; opponents of the Tories

CHRONOLOGY

1639 Increase Mather is born June 21 in Dorchester, Massachusetts.

1651 Enters Harvard College at the age of 12.

1656 Graduates with bachelor of arts degree.

1657 Preaches first sermon; sails for Ireland and England; attends Trinity College in Dublin.

1658 Receives master of arts degree from Trinity College.

1661 After brief stays at Weymouth and Dorchester in Dorset, England, returns to Boston.

1662 Marries Maria Cotton.

1663 Cotton Mather is born to Maria and Increase.

1664 Becomes teacher of the Second Church, Boston.

1685 Appointed acting president of Harvard College.

1688 Selected as envoy of Congregational churches of Massachusetts Bay Colony to restore the charter revoked by James II.

1692 Returns to Boston with Royal Governor William Phips.

1693 Opposes the methods of spectral evidence in the Salem Witch Trials.

1701 Resigns as president of Harvard.

1714 Maria dies.

1723 Increase Mather dies in Boston on August 23.

COLONIAL TIME LINE

1607 Jamestown, Virginia, is settled by the English.

1620 Pilgrims on the *Mayflower* land at Plymouth, Massachusetts.

1623 The Dutch settle New Netherlands, the colony that later becomes New York.

1630 Massachusetts Bay Colony is started.

1634 Maryland is settled as a Roman Catholic colony. Later Maryland becomes a safe place for people with different religious beliefs.

1636 Roger Williams is thrown out of the Massachusetts Bay Colony. He settles Rhode Island, the first colony to give people freedom of religion.

1682 William Penn forms the colony of Pennsylvania.

1688 Pennsylvania Quakers make the first formal protest against slavery.

1692 Trials for witchcraft are held in Salem, Massachusetts.

1712 Slaves revolt in New York. Twenty-one blacks are killed as punishment.

1720 Major smallpox outbreak occurs in Boston. Cotton Mather and some doctors try a new treatment. Many people think the new treatment shouldn't be used.

1754 French and Indian War begins. It ends nine years later.

1761 Benjamin Banneker builds a wooden clock that keeps precise time.

1765 Britain passes the Stamp Act. Violent protests break out in the colonies. The Stamp Act is ended the next year.

1775 The battles of Lexington and Concord begin the American Revolution.

1776 Declaration of Independence is signed.

FURTHER READING

Collier, Christopher. *Pilgrims and Puritans*. New York: Benchmark Books, 1998.

Doherty, Kieran. *William Bradford: The Rock of Plymouth*. Brookfield, CT: Twenty-First Century Books, 1999.

Hering, Marianne. *William Bradford: Governor of Plymouth Colony*. Philadelphia: Chelsea House Publishers, 2000.

Lutz, Norma Jean. *Cotton Mather: Author, Clergyman, and Scholar*. Philadelphia: Chelsea House Publishers, 2000.

Mexaxas, Eric. *Squanto and the Miracle of Thanksgiving*. Nashville, TN: Tommy Nelson, 1999.

Waters, Kate. *On the Mayflower*. New York: Scholastic, 1996.

INDEX

INDEX

PICTURE CREDITS

page

3: Archive Photos

6: Archive Photos

13: Archive Photos

16: Archive Photos

18: Historical Picture Archive/
Corbis

23: Richard T. Nowitz/Corbis

27: Victoria & Albert Museum,
London/Art Resource, NY

30: Burstein Collection/Corbis

41: Farrell Grehan/Corbis

43: Archive Photos

44: The Newark Museum/
Art Resource, NY

46: Archive Photos

49: Bettmann/Corbis

53: Hulton Getty Collection/
Archive Photos

54: Archive Photos

61: Archive Photos

64: Archive Photos

ABOUT THE AUTHOR

NORMA JEAN LUTZ, who lives in Tulsa, Oklahoma, has been writing professionally since 1977. She is the author of more than 250 short stories and articles as well as 39 books—fiction and nonfiction. Of all the writing she does, she most enjoys writing children's books.

Senior Consulting Editor **ARTHUR M. SCHLESINGER, JR.** is the leading American historian of our time. He won the Pulitzer Prize for his book *The Age of Jackson* (1945) and again for *A Thousand Days* (1965). This chronicle of the Kennedy Administration also won a National Book Award. He has written many other books including a multi-volume series, *The Age of Roosevelt*. Professor Schlesinger is the Albert Schweitzer Professor of the Humanities at the City University of New York, and has been involved in several other Chelsea House projects, including the REVOLUTIONARY WAR LEADERS biographies on the most prominent figures of early American history.